UP CLOSE

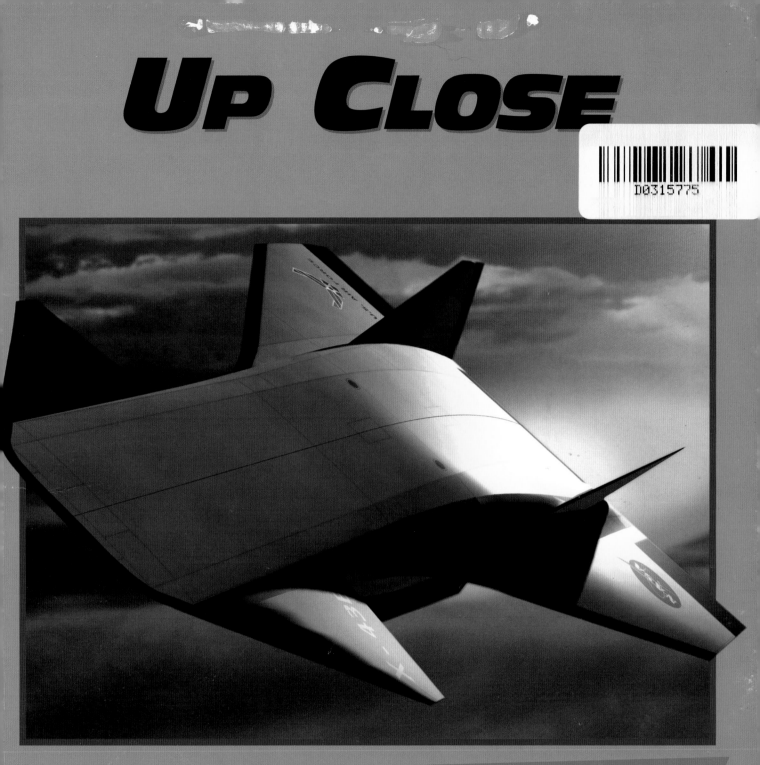

SPEED
MACHINES

PAUL HARRISON

W
FRANKLIN WATTS
LONDON · SYDNEY

Published in 2008 by Franklin Watts
Reprinted in 2010

Copyright © 2008 Arcturus Publishing Limited

Franklin Watts
338 Euston Road
London NW1 3BH

Franklin Watts Australia
Level 17/207 Kent Street
Sydney NSW 2000

Author: Paul Harrison
Designer (new edition): Silvie Rabbe
Editor (new edition): Fiona Tulloch

Picture credits: Corbis: page 3, bottom; page 4, bottom; page 6; page 11, top; Empics: page 13, top; Getty: page 8, bottom; page 9, bottom; page 11, bottom; page 16;

Science Photo Library: title page; page 2, bottom; page 3, top and middle; page 5, bottom right; page 9, top; page 15, top and bottom.

A CIP catalogue record for this book is available from the British Library

Dewey number: 629

ISBN: 978-1-4451-0129-3
SL000949EN

Printed in China

Franklin Watts is a division of Hachette Children's Books, an Hachette UK Company
www.hachette.co.uk

Contents

Up and Away

T oday we travel at speeds that were unthinkable a hundred years ago. On land and through the air, we use clever machines to help us move very quickly indeed. Here are some of the fastest ones.

SPEEDY

The speed of sound is measured as 1159 km per hour and is known as "Mach 1". The first plane to travel this fast was Bell X-1, in 1947. Amazing, as the first plane was only invented in 1903!

THE WINNER

The Helios space probes are the fastest machines in the world. They travel at 245,270 km per hour! They have set the record for being the closest manmade objects to the Sun at just 45 million km away.

The Space Shuttle goes from 0 to 27,358 km per hour in just eight minutes.

BLAST OFF!

Shuttles weigh 2 million kg at lift-off and are 37 metres long. To launch this huge weight, they have very powerful engines.

Speedier Than

S ince the Wright Brothers first invented the aeroplane, air travel has become more and more advanced. It shows no signs of slowing down, either.

A sonic boom is the loud noise made when a plane breaks the speed of sound.

NASA
831

BATTLE IN THE SKY

Military fighter planes attack other aircraft. They are small and can fly 3000 km per hour.

Sound

SNEAKY

The fastest jet plane is the SR-71 Blackbird, which has travelled at Mach 3.2. This is over three times the speed of sound. It was built as a spy plane because it was *supersonic* and could fly very high in the air. This makes it hard to detect.

SLOW COACH

The fastest passenger plane ever was Concorde. It is no longer used, so people can only travel at 800 km per hour.

Wonders on

B efore the 1800s, the only way for people to travel more quickly was to ride a horse. Then along came the age of steam and the invention of the train.

SLOW BEGINNINGS

The first steam train was designed in 1804 by a Cornishman called Richard Trevithick. It moved along rather well—at 8 km per hour!

STEAMING PAST

Steam trains soon began flying down the rails. The fastest steam train ever was the Mallard. It reached top speeds of 202 km per hour.

Rails

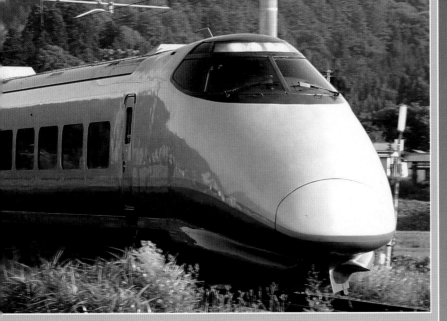

SPEEDING BULLET

The Shinkansen is the Japanese bullet train. In everyday use it reaches speeds of 360 km per hour! Over one billion people have used it.

The first passengers were worried they would move too quickly to breathe!

ZOOM!

The French TGV (which stands for "train à grande vitesse") is powered by electricity. It holds the rail land speed record.

4512

Boy Racers

The first car was invented in 1885 and chugged along at not much beyond walking pace. Nowadays there are more cars than ever before and loads of different ways to race them.

QUICK

Formula One's Grand Prix races are the most famous of all motor sports. The cars are *aerodynamic* and powerful, allowing them to travel from 0 to 100 km per hour in 2.5 seconds!

Tyres without treads give the most grip as more rubber touches the road.

WHAT A DRAG

You might think Formula One cars are the fastest vehicles in motor sport—but they're not! *Dragsters* are by far the quickest. They go over 500 km per hour and need parachutes as well as brakes to slow down properly.

GOING ON TOUR

Touring cars look like normal cars but have much more powerful engines and brakes. Championships are very popular in Britain and America.

DRAG ACT

There's a motorbike version of every racing car. Scrambling bikes do the same job as rally cars. Quad bikes are versions of off-road cars. But drag bikes do the high-speed racing. The fastest drag bikes cover a 400-metre track in just over six seconds.

Drag bikes are quicker than Thrust SSC, the car that holds the land speed record.

DARING BUT DEADLY

The two-wheeled version of Formula One is called Moto GP. Motorbike racing is skilful and very dangerous. There's nothing between the rider and the road!

ON YOUR BIKE

It doesn't look like a motorbike, but it is! The BUB Enterprise Streamliner set the world motorbike land speed record in 2006. Its top measured speed was 564 km per hour.

15

Watery Wonders

For some daredevils, rowing a boat or riding on a ferry isn't enough. They need to get their kicks with some high-speed water action!

BUMPY RIDE

It is difficult to move through water quickly because boats have to push their way through it. Offshore powerboats have the fastest *velocity*, because they skim across the top of the water. They can reach up to 273 km per hour.

HIGH PRICE TO PAY

In 1967, Donald Campbell's attempt to beat the water speed record went badly wrong. His boat lifted out of the water, spun through the air and broke up as it hit the water. He died instantly.

The first boat awarded the Blue Riband took over 18.5 days to cross the Atlantic.

FASTEST EVER

The speediest boat around is called Spirit of Australia. It set the water speed record ~~~ in 1978. The jet-powered ~~~ along at 511.13 km

The Future of

I t has been several years since the speed records were broken. Have we reached our limit or will we develop newer, even quicker machines in the future?

FRICTION-FREE

Friction is a slowing effect that occurs when one thing touches another. Trains can avoid this by using magnets that hover above a rail while an electric charge pushes the train along. They can go up to 580 km per hour!

Speed

SCRAM!

NASA is developing the world's quickest aeroplane called the X-43 Scramjet. It travels at around 11,265 kilometres per hour.

The Scramjet will fly at 15 times the speed of sound.

SUNNY SIDE UP

Scientists think we will run out of petrol and oil in as little as 50 years' time. Solar-powered vehicles are not very fast yet, but they may become the speed machines of the future.

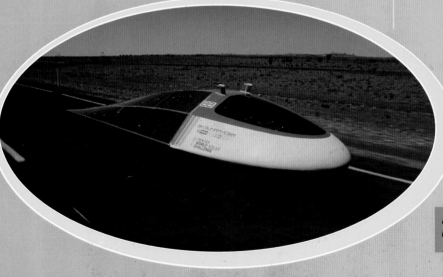

WALKING TALL

In the future, we can just make ourselves move quicker. Attaching velocity stilts to your legs makes you run at 50 km per hour!

Glossary

ACCELERATE
To begin to move quickly.

AERODYNAMIC
Designed to reduce wind drag and increase speed.

DRAGSTER
A vehicle specially built for drag racing.

FRICTION
The resistance that an object encounters when moving over another object.

SOUND BARRIER
An imaginary barrier at the speed of sound (1223 km per hour).

SUPERSONIC
Capable of reaching speeds beyond the speed of sound.

VELOCITY
High-speed motion or action.

Further Reading

Record Breakers and Other Speed Machines
Moira Butterfield, Keith Harmer & Chris Grigg, Scholastic, 1995

Speed Machines (Mission Extreme 3D)
John Starke, Red Bird Publishing, 2004

Speed Machines (Pop-Up Books)
Sue Whiting, Book Company Publishing, 2002

Speed Machines Inside and Out
Steve Parker, Heinemann, 2006

The Best Book Of Speed Machines
Ian Graham, Kingfisher, 2002

Index